KING ARTHUR

KING ARTHUR

⊰ ‡ ⊱

HOW HISTORY IS INVENTED

Jeremy Roberts

LERNER PUBLICATIONS COMPANY
MINNEAPOLIS

Lerner Publications Company
A division of Lerner Publishing Group
241 First Avenue North
Minneapolis, MN 55401 U.S.A.

Website address: www.lernerbooks.com

Library of Congress Cataloging-in-Publication Data

Roberts, Jeremy, 1956–
    King Arthur / by Jeremy Roberts.
      p.   cm. — (How history is invented)
    Summary: Examines both the legends and the facts surrounding the
literary and historical figure of Britain's King Arthur.
    ISBN 0-8225-4891-7 (lib. bdg. : alk. paper)
    1. Arthur, King—Juvenile literature. 2. Great Britain—Antiquities,
Celtic—Juvenile literature. 3. Great Britain—History—To 1066—
Juvenile literature. 4. Arthurian Romances—Sources—Juvenile
literature. 5. Britons—Kings and Rulers—Juvenile literature.
[1. Arthur, King. 2. Arthur, King—Legends. 3. Kings, queens,
rulers, etc. 4. Great Britain—History—To 1066.] I. Title. II. Series.
DA152.5.A7. 67   2001
942.01'4—dc21   00-008875

Manufactured in the United States of America
1 2 3 4 5 6 – JR – 06 05 04 03 02 01

CONTENTS

——⁂ ✝ ⁂——

A NOTE ON SPELLING

The names of the various characters associated with Arthur have been spelled in a variety of different ways over the centuries. To give just one example, Merlin is most commonly spelled with an *i*, but it is spelled with a *y* in Thomas Malory's text, the most famous and complete telling of the legend.

I have tried to use the most common spellings. When in doubt, I have followed the spellings in Richard Barber's 1986 book, *King Arthur, Hero and Legend* (New York: St. Martin's Press), which appeals to both scholarly and popular audiences. In a few cases where it might be overly confusing—most notably the spelling of Igrayne, which is rendered as Igerna and Ygerne elsewhere—I have resorted to Malory's spelling, since that is the primary source.

WHO'S WHO

There are many different stories and legends about King Arthur and his knights. The authors don't always agree on who did what, or even how to spell different names. Here are some of the more important characters in the tales, along with what most authors say about them.

Arthur *(AHR-thur)*—
historic and legendary king. In the legends, he is the once and future king of England and the founder of the Round Table.

Sir Ector *(EHK-tohr)*—
the nobleman who raises Arthur as his son and first realizes that he is king

Sir Galahad *(GAL-ah-had)*—
Sir Lancelot's son. He finds the Holy Grail.

Sir Gawain *(GAH-wayn or GAH-wihn)*—
Arthur's nephew and one of the greatest knights of the Round Table. He appears in Geoffrey of Monmouth's tale.

Guenevere *(GWEHN-ih-veer)*—
Arthur's wife. Probably only a legendary or fictional character, but some scholars believe she is based on a real queen. Guenevere's name is often spelled Guinevere. It also appears as Gwenhwyfar, Gwenhumare, and Gnevra.

Sir Kay *(KAY)*—
Arthur's stepbrother and one of the first knights of the Round Table

Sir Lancelot *(LAN-suh-laht)*—
the greatest knight of the Round Table. He betrays Arthur by having an affair with the queen.

Merlin *(MUR-lihn)*—
a magician and seer, or prophet. He is an important adviser to Arthur and Arthur's father, Uther Pendragon.

Mordred *(MOHR-drehd)*—
Arthur's son, conceived with his half sister Morgause. (In some versions of the story, he is simply Arthur's nephew.) Mordred takes over Arthur's kingdom after Lancelot's betrayal. He gravely wounds Arthur in their final battle.

Morgause *(MOHR-gouz)*—
Arthur's half sister, wife of King Lot, and mother of Gawain, Mordred, and three other boys. While under a magic spell, Arthur fell in love with her.

Uther Pendragon *(YOO-thur PEHN-dra-gohn)*—
Arthur's father

King Arthur of Britain

—— ✦ ONE ✦ ——

KING FOREVER

T HE WARRIOR SAT ON HIS HORSE AS THE MORNING mist drifted across the hills of southern England. A short distance away lay his enemies, fierce Saxons who had been raiding his homeland for one hundred years or more. The Saxons had once lived in northwestern Germany and Denmark. They had raided and conquered much of northern Europe over the past two hundred years and then crossed the English Channel, looking for land and plunder. Finally they had reached the warrior's homeland in the British Isles. If the Saxons were not defeated soon, the warrior and his people would be driven into the sea.

He had gathered an army from kings and chieftains all across the land. The soldiers behind him prepared for battle, readying horses and sharpening swords and lances. The men were from different tribes and clans. But they had vowed to fight as a single force to preserve their land and that of their neighbors. They considered the Saxons to be barbarians and thieves.

The Saxons were not the only dark cloud that hung over the island, nor the only problem creasing the leader's brow. Since Julius Caesar had conquered England around 55 B.C., the Roman Empire—through

Ruins like those shown above are reminders of the Roman presence in Britain centuries ago.

its excellent army, strong leaders, and rule of law—had brought stability to the land for hundreds of years. But the empire had been crumbling for two generations as various Germanic chiefs attacked it and carved it into many different kingdoms. Little more than its roads were left in this land far from Rome. Many minor kings and leaders, who often opposed each other, ruled and defended England. They were of different backgrounds and races, and they lacked a leader who could unite them.

Clad in thick leather armor and well armed with daring and cunning, the warrior on horseback was determined to be that leader. He had already defeated the Saxons in several battles, but on this day in the early A.D. 500s he would face his greatest challenge.

Somewhere between one thousand and two thousand Saxons, all on foot, opposed him. His army was no larger, but his men were on horses. He had learned to use mobility as a weapon, and he took advantage of the geography of rivers and streams as he planned his battles. If God allowed, he would win a victory so momentous that peace would reign for a generation. For years to come, men would talk of this hill—Badon—and the battle fought here.

At least, he prayed this would be the case. The sun was rising, and the day would soon tell his fate.

The man on horseback might well have been hopeful, but not in his wildest imagination could he have predicted how great and momentous his victory would be. Nor would he have dared guess how far his fame would spread, nor how much honor would be heaped on him. He certainly could not know that his name would live on fifteen hundred years after his death or that it would become a synonym for bravery and leadership.

His name was a simple one: Arthur. Soon after that day, he would be called king—for now and forever.

This portrayal of the Round Table, where legends say King Arthur and his knights dined, is displayed in Winchester, England.

---— ♊ TWO ♊ —---

HISTORY AND LEGEND

T HE LEGEND OF KING ARTHUR HAS GROWN tremendously since that distant battle. The legendary King Arthur is known as the greatest king who ever lived. He is said to have ruled a kingdom called Camelot with his wife Guenevere. The world's greatest knights were members of his court. They did many good deeds and went on quests, or adventures. They were all equal and sat at a round table to show that no one had a higher rank than another. The most famous knights, such as Sir Gawain and Sir Lancelot, saved maidens in distress and searched for a precious chalice, or cup, called the Holy Grail. They were brave heroes, though they had faults like all of us.

In the legends, Arthur is the perfect knight, with flashing swords and impressive armor. Aided by the magic of Merlin the wizard, Arthur defeats many enemies. He has two magic swords. At the beginning of his reign, he pulls one from a block of stone, an act that proves he is the true king. The other sword appears in the middle of a lake and has powers that make Arthur almost immortal. At the end of his reign, Arthur returns to the lake and disappears into the mist.

Arthur is the once and future king of Britain, destined to return to Britain to rule again. He is also a bold hero who symbolizes, or represents, the best of the Middle Ages (A.D. 500 to the fifteenth century)—and of our time as well. Many books, poems, and stories have been written about King Arthur, his knights, and the Round Table. Many movies have been made about them. *The Sword in the Stone*, for example, tells of King Arthur's discovery that he is king. *Merlin* deals with the magician who helped Arthur rule. *First Knight* tells the story of Lancelot, Arthur's friend, who unfortunately becomes his greatest enemy. In all of these tales, Arthur and his knights fight bravely. They fight for justice and truth, and they almost always win.

But are these stories true? Was King Arthur a real person? Did he really live in Britain? If so, where was Camelot? Was his wife, Guenevere, real? Was she the most beautiful woman who ever lived? What about Arthur's knights? How close are the legends to provable facts?

Historians aren't sure. For many centuries, they knew that the legends about him had been invented. Because of that, many thought Arthur had been invented by writers, too. They have only recently realized that Arthur may have truly existed.

These are the facts about Arthur that most historians believe: Arthur probably did exist. He was probably a king, or at least a great leader, somewhere in the area of what became Great Britain, which includes England, Wales, and Scotland. He led an army against the Saxons in the distant past and won a glorious victory.

Most historians also believe that Arthur lived around the end of the fifth and the beginning of the sixth centuries A.D. They also agree that he was the inspiration for thousands of tales and histories.

Beyond that, though, there is little agreement about Arthur. History and legend, fact and fiction, have intertwined in the many years since the battle at Badon.

Ironies

It may seem strange, but the legends that made Arthur famous are part of the problem in learning about the "real," or historical, Arthur.

Picts

Edinburgh

NORTH
SEA

N

Scots

ISLE OF
MAN

IRISH
OCEAN

Wales

Angles

Britons

BRISTOL
CHANNEL

London

Bath

STONEHENGE

Tintagel

Britons

CADBURY
CASTLE

Winchester

Saxons

ISLE OF
WIGHT

ENGLISH CHANNEL

ATLANTIC
OCEAN

Arthurian
England

While the legends boast of a magnificent castle such as this one, the historical King Arthur's castle probably wasn't as grand.

The legends seem to tell us much about Arthur, but the way they describe him makes it difficult to separate fact from fiction. There are many obvious exaggerations. For example, no one could have won so many sword fights without being killed or wounded. And the magic of Merlin, Arthur's friend and adviser, seems too fantastic to be true.

However, we easily accept many other parts of the tales, such as the notion that Arthur lived in Camelot, a magnificent stone castle with a vast moat and grand towers, or that he dressed in a fine suit of fancy plate armor. But historians tell us that such castles and armor didn't exist in Arthur's time. In fact, they developed about the same time that most popular tales about Arthur were being written—

hundreds of years after he had died. Military fortifications during the historical Arthur's day were probably reinforced dirt and stone walls rather than fine stone castles. Leather and sometimes chain mail were used as armor, but plate metal hadn't been invented.

Most of the stories about Arthur talk about chivalry. Chivalry is the code of knightly conduct. It governs everything King Arthur and his knights do in many of the legends. A chivalrous person respects others. He allows his enemy to live after surrendering. We still believe in some parts of the code of chivalry—or at least think that it is an honorable code of behavior. Arthur and the code of chivalry seem inseparable in people's minds.

The code of chivalry actually evolved long after his death, just like castles and fancy armor. At the end of the fifth and beginning of the sixth century, Arthur's code of conduct would have been much different. It would seem harsh from our modern viewpoint. Women were not treated with what we would consider respect, for example, and an enemy could not expect mercy in battle under any circumstances.

There are countless other differences between the image of Arthur that is portrayed in the legends and the historical Arthur, the man on horseback awaiting the Saxon charge. We know the legendary Arthur much better than we know the real hero.

And yet they are the same person—or at least different versions of the same person. The two Arthurs occasionally come together, and it has become almost impossible to see one without thinking about the other.

In 1952 researchers unearthed Saxon remains during excavation work in Canterbury, England.

---— ❧ THREE ❧ —---

THE HISTORICAL RECORD

L ONG AFTER THE MIDDLE AGES HAD ENDED, PEOPLE were still interested in Arthur and the stories about him. But by that time, attitudes toward history had changed. Modern scholars specialize in history and use scientific methods, such as archaeology and textual analysis, to separate fact from fiction.

For years, many historians believed King Arthur was a fictional character who had never really existed and that the stories about him had been spun from thin air. They thought there was not enough proof of a historical Arthur. There were no bones, no grave, no monument from his time with his name on it. Even the few historians who believed the legends were based on a real person admitted to having some doubts. More information existed about dinosaurs than the real King Arthur.

Gradually, some historians began to make discoveries that convinced most scholars that Arthur was real. They used methods such as archaeology (digging in the ground for the remains of old structures and battlefields), but they mostly studied texts. Some of these texts mentioned Arthur directly, but others didn't. By comparing the texts, scholars were able to gather valuable clues about who Arthur was and what he had done.

In some cases, historians had to make guesses and interpret the evidence they had. They pieced together clues like detectives and based their interpretations on other facts they knew. Sometimes they tried to make analogies, or comparisons, when interpreting. They sifted through the legends, looking for clues about the historic Arthur. Finally, they were able to determine that Arthur was real, but questions remain about who he was and what he did.

First Appearances

One of Arthur's first appearances in literature was in a history written by a man called Nennius. He lived in Wales, which is next to England in southwestern Great Britain, and he wrote during the early ninth century. His work was called *Historia Britonum,* or *History of the Britons.* Arthur is briefly mentioned as a great leader. Nennius says Arthur brought the kings of Britain together and won impressive battles against the Saxons.

Although Nennius called the book a "history," we probably wouldn't consider it much of a history if it were written in modern times. We'd think it was fiction, like a novel or even a fairy tale. Nennius includes two "marvels," or miracles, to prove Arthur's greatness, but both seem more like fairy tales or superstitions. One is about the tomb of Arthur's dog. Stones were piled on the grave. Supposedly a stone with the dog's paw print always rose to the top of the pile, no matter how many stones were placed on top of it. The other marvel is about a grave whose dimensions cannot be accurately measured by anyone. The grave belongs to Arthur's son, Mordred. Nennius says Arthur killed him, but does not explain why.

Arthur and his battle against the Saxons are mentioned in the *Annales Cambriae,* or *Annals of Wales.* The *Annals* list events that took place over a period of 553 years. It's a little like a timeline of the past. Unfortunately, the years are numbered from "1," and historians are not sure what year 1 is on our calendar. Many believe year 1 equals the year A.D. 447, but there is debate about this.

Historians do know that the version of the *Annals* they have was put together after the eighth century, long after many of the recorded events

King Arthur defeats the Saxons at Badon.

occurred. While that doesn't mean the *Annals* are mistaken, it does raise questions about the book's accuracy.

Still, there is valuable information about Arthur in the *Annals*. One entry notes a battle that Arthur won at Badon. It also says that he wore a Christian cross on his shield. Another entry says Arthur died nineteen years after Badon.

At first, historians looked at these reports skeptically. The works raised so many questions that the historians didn't think any of the information in them could be true. Magic stones? Who would believe that? But as historians studied the texts more closely, they began to believe that the *Annals* and *Historia Britonum* actually do explain much about the historical Arthur. For example, these two works tell us that Arthur won such a great battle that it was remembered for hundreds of years. At a time when very little was being recorded, Arthur's victory was noteworthy. People talked and wrote about the victory for centuries. The details became hazy, but the battle must have been important at the time.

The work of Nennius and the *Annals* also have clues we can use to make guesses about who Arthur was. For example, if he had a Christian cross on his shield, it would be likely that Arthur was a Christian. And his name is the kind of name someone who had Roman ancestors might have. But the most important clue that these sources give about Arthur is the name of his enemy: the Saxons.

Historians do know that the Saxons invaded Britain during the 400s and the 500s, and they know where and when some of their battles took place. Historians also have a good idea when the battle of Badon occurred. There are some differing opinions about the exact date, but it is usually recorded as A.D. 516. Historians can also date some of the other entries in the *Annals* and connect them with facts about Arthur. For these and other reasons, historians believe Arthur lived around the year 500.

Stock Hero

Besides being mentioned in Nennius's work and the *Annals of Wales*, Arthur makes several brief, tantalizing appearances in different writings before the twelfth century. In some he appears as a stock hero—just another good guy battling the bad guys.

Arthur also appears in several biographies of the saints. A Welsh collection of tales, *The Mabinogion*, includes one story with Arthur in it. Historians believe the tale dates from the tenth century or even earlier. All the stories are about heroes and myths.

Arthur is also a character in some British stories written after the twelfth century. These tales are similar to French stories written at about the same time. Because of that similarity, some scholars believe the stories are based on older texts that have been lost. Scholars think that in both the French and British stories, the writers used an earlier text to inspire them. It was very common in those days to rewrite or retell older stories, and it would have been odd for people in places far apart to think of the same story at the same time.

There are no records surviving from Arthur's court. There are no letters from him, no orders to his troops, not even a bill with his name on it. But this is not surprising. The period during which Arthur lived was a traumatic one in British history, filled with invasions and bloodshed. Even if such records had been kept, it is easy to understand how they could have been lost. But they probably never existed. The way we know about Arthur—through stories written long after he might have lived—would fit with that historical period.

Turmoil and Oral Tales

Why were the first stories about Arthur written so long after he lived, and where did they come from? Historians say that great turmoil occurred in Britain around A.D. 500. The powerful Romans had conquered the island hundreds of years earlier, but in the fifth century, the Roman Empire began to crumble. The Roman government ordered its armies and government officials to return to the European continent, closer to home. In their place, local lords and chieftains vied, or competed, for power. They formed their own armies and kept order. Some chieftains were descendants of Romans. Others were descendants of the Celts, the people Rome had conquered.

At about the same time, Germanic tribes began to invade and then settle in Britain. The Saxons were among these people. Their customs were different from those of the other inhabitants. Conflicts over land and resources led to fighting and war.

Unfortunately, we don't have much written information about the battles that took place or even about everyday life at that time. People then had a different view than we have about history and how it should be recorded. Many people couldn't read or write, and they were not very interested in specific dates.

Instead of writing, people put information about kings and famous leaders into songs and poems. The songs and poems were memorized and passed down from generation to generation, creating an oral tradition. At feasts, celebrations, and other special occasions, people performed the most elaborate tales from memory. This method is excellent for passing down deeds and occurrences that people want to remember, either because they're wonderful or horrible. Because they're not written, however, the stories tend to change from teller to teller. It's a little like the old-fashioned game "telephone." As each

People gather around a bard, who tells about famous historical events through poems and songs.

person in the circle whispers a sentence to the next person, the sentence changes slightly. By the end of the game, the sentence is often very different from the original one.

Stories in an oral tradition are often written down long after they were first composed. When historians study them, they have to determine what's factual and what isn't. Sometimes oral traditions can be remarkably accurate. Historians can use other evidence to verify or add to the information in these records. At other times, however, no verifiable information is available.

The early written accounts of Arthur seem to be based on an oral tradition. They may come from earlier oral records or reports that were prepared while Arthur was alive. These early accounts include not only battles but also magic and Christian symbols. This is what one would expect if the stories had been composed during Arthur's life and times.

Historians feel confident that there is some truth behind the early accounts, but they still have many questions. For example, why isn't Arthur mentioned in other writings that record the same events? Why is Arthur given credit for things historians know he couldn't have done? And why can't historians find all the places where Arthur's battles took place?

These questions may never be answered. Admittedly, what we know about Arthur's time remains very sketchy, and some historians remain skeptical. However, most historians are convinced there was an Arthur, that he did lead British troops in battle, and that he did win a resounding victory. Beyond that, legend begins.

Merlin, a wizard, is said to have helped King Arthur build a great empire.

FOUR

GEOFFREY OF MONMOUTH:
LEGEND GROWS FROM HISTORY

ONCE THERE WAS A FABULOUS YOUNG MAN, *stronger and bolder than anyone who had ever lived. He was a natural leader, the son of a great king. He was wise and ambitious, and his name was Arthur.*

Arthur was crowned king at a young age, succeeding his father— another wise and wonderful man. Arthur went on to defeat the Saxons in the battles mentioned by the great historian Nennius. He married a beautiful woman, and with the help of magic and a wizard named Merlin, he built a grand empire. He left England and conquered Europe, fighting the entire Roman Empire. Not even Rome could stand up to him, and Arthur defeated the emperor and his armies.

But just then word came from England that Mordred, the man he had left in charge of his kingdom, had taken over. Arthur rushed back home. There, Arthur and Mordred did battle. Their final battle was ferocious. Many men were killed, including Mordred.

Although Arthur won the battle, he had been fatally wounded. He appointed a kinsman to rule in his place. Then he was taken to a special place called Avalon, but what happened there, no one can truly say.

This is the outline of Arthur's life as told by Geoffrey of Monmouth. He wrote the story of Arthur in a book called *Historia Regum Britanniae*, or *The History of the Kings of Britain*, around 1136. It is the oldest telling of Arthur's complete life and death that we have, and Geoffrey wrote it as a true and accurate history of the real Arthur.

Geoffrey of Monmouth

Geoffrey lived from about 1100 to 1154. Monmouth is a town in southeastern Wales. Since it was attached to Geoffrey's name, most historians believe that is where he came from.

Like many other scholars at the time, Geoffrey worked for the Catholic Church most of his life. The church was one of the few institutions that valued learning during the Middle Ages. It was also a large, powerful institution. It established colleges and universities, and many writers and historians were connected to the church in some way.

A fortified bridge in Monmouth, Wales

Geoffrey was ordained (officially became a priest) in 1152 and soon afterward became a bishop. But his main interest seems to have been writing, learning, and teaching. He was at Oxford, England's first university, from 1129 to 1151. Geoffrey is thought to be of Celtic descent. His *History* was the most famous of his many works.

Geoffrey set out to write a history of Britain dating back to ancient times. Arthur is just one of the kings Geoffrey writes about, though in many ways he seems the greatest king. Geoffrey claimed he translated the Arthur story from a Welsh text he received from a friend named Walter of Oxford, the provost of the college and archdeacon of the city. Some historians think this may be true, but they have been unable to find the Welsh book. However, Geoffrey may have said this just to make his own book seem more convincing.

Geoffrey wrote in the days before printing presses, when manuscripts were laboriously copied by hand. People rarely owned books, unless they were wealthy or members of the church hierarchy. Nonetheless, Geoffrey's work was extremely popular—the Middle Ages equivalent of a best-seller.

Geoffrey's book is presented as true, but we have learned that much of what is written is either inaccurate or pure invention. For example, Geoffrey seems to have been mistaken about the names of many places he wrote about. That does not mean, however, that everything he wrote is fiction or that Geoffrey even knew that his history was inaccurate.

The sections on Arthur begin with Arthur's father, Uther Pendragon, and then follow Arthur to his death. Geoffrey repeats and embellishes, or adds to, information from Nennius and also refers to the early Welsh tales. Geoffrey introduces Merlin the wizard to the story. Merlin, with his gifts of prophecy and magic, helps Uther and Arthur. Geoffrey writes about Arthur's wife, Guenevere. He also says that Mordred was a villain and writes about him in detail. Although Mordred is mentioned in the *Annals,* the reference doesn't make clear whether he is Arthur's friend or foe.

Geoffrey's tale is long compared to earlier accounts of Arthur, but it leaves many questions unanswered. For example, Geoffrey tells us

Oxford is the oldest university in Britain. Pictured above is one of its oldest colleges, All Souls College in Oxfordshire.

that Arthur was badly hurt but does not say if Aurthur actually died from his wound. And although Geoffrey claims his book is a history, the Arthur tale includes many accounts we know are not true. For example, no English king fought against a Roman emperor in Europe, as Geoffrey claims. Because of this, we know we cannot trust all of Geoffrey's tale as fact.

The story is important for many reasons, however. First of all, Geoffrey's information about the historical Arthur may have come from earlier writings that no longer exist, so his book serves as a starting point for anyone investigating the historical Arthur. Geoffrey's tale is even more important for anyone interested in the legendary Arthur, because the Arthur legend begins with Geoffrey. His "history" gave birth to great fictions.

Most of the writers who followed Geoffrey took what he wrote and then added their own details and sense of style, embellishing his story and going beyond it. In many ways, Arthur the legend became more interesting and entertaining than the historical king. Arthur the legend was a great king, fighting in many battles not mentioned in the earlier histories. As a legend, he possessed many qualities the historic Arthur may or may not have had. After all, a legendary person can do many things a real person cannot do.

Although Geoffrey's work was presented as true, a few people questioned it even then. That did not prevent them from wanting to hear more about Arthur, however. They wanted to know about his court, his achievements, and where he came from. Poets and other writers soon began giving Arthur's story more details, and the legend quickly mushroomed.

Tintagel Castle at Cornwall is said to have belonged to King Arthur.

FIVE

THE LEGEND:
ARTHUR'S FIRST DAYS

THIS IS A SUMMARY OF THE STORY OF ARTHUR'S early years, as told by Sir Thomas Malory. Malory is considered the greatest English Arthurian writer. He wrote in 1470, centuries after Geoffrey, and he seems to have combined several different accounts of Arthur's life. He also added some details of his own. Except for the fact that Arthur existed, little in Malory's tale is true, but it is still a great story that shows just how fantastic the legend became.

In the dark days of Britain, war was widespread, and sword often crashed against sword. According to the legends, Uther Pendragon, king of England, lived at this time.

The king had been at war with a great leader of Cornwall, the Duke of Tintagel. Cornwall is in southwest England, near the sea. When they made peace, Uther asked the duke and his wife, Igrayne, to come to his castle. While there, the duke's wife soon realized that Uther was in love with her. She told the duke, and they fled in the middle of the night, returning to the duke's castle.

Uther was angry at Tintagel for leaving so abruptly, since it was a great insult. But more important, he lusted for Igrayne and would do anything to have her.

He decided to wage war against the duke and attack his great castles, hoping to take Igrayne for his own. He sent for Merlin, the greatest magician in the land. Merlin said he would help him, but on one condition: the king must give him the child he would have with Igrayne. "It shall be to your worship's and to the child's benefit," said Merlin, but he added no explanation.

When the king agreed, Merlin cast a spell disguising Uther as the duke. Uther went that night to the castle. Fooled by the spell, Igrayne made love to him. In the morning, the disguised king left.

When Igrayne heard that her husband had died in battle the day before, she was shocked and unsure what had happened. She knew she hadn't imagined it, since she was pregnant. She believed it was her husband—yet that was impossible.

As Merlin had predicted, Uther's forces vanquished the duke's army and captured his castles. Uther quickly married Igrayne. When he asked about the child she was expecting, the queen told him the entire story. Uther smiled, explaining the mystery. Igrayne, now in love with the king, was happy to know it was his child.

But her happiness ended when the boy was born, because Merlin appeared and demanded that the king give him his son as he had agreed. Uther handed the child to Merlin, and the magician spirited him away to be raised by Sir Ector, a worthy knight, and his wife.

Only Merlin knew of Arthur's royal birth. King Uther died a short while later, poisoned by the treachery of his kingdom's greatest enemies, the Saxons.

Without a king or heir, the country was plunged into chaos, as different rivals vied for the throne without success. Finally, a stone with an anvil and sword appeared in a churchyard. On it were written the words, "Whoso pulleth this sword out of this stone and anvil is the rightfully born king of all England." Many dukes and lords tried but failed to pull the sword from its stone.

Besides Arthur, Sir Ector had a son named Kay. Raised as brothers,

Merlin takes baby Arthur into his keeping.

the two boys were very close. When Kay was first made a knight, Arthur served him as a squire. It happened that soon after Kay was knighted, he and Arthur attended a jousting tournament near the great sword. Many great knights, dressed in lavish suits of armor with bright cloths waving as their pennants, took part. Before he was to enter into the competition, Kay realized he had forgotten his sword and asked Arthur to fetch it. Arthur searched and couldn't find it, but he was determined that his brother be armed. When Arthur saw the sword in the stone, he ran to it and drew it from the anvil.

Sir Ector recognized the sword as Arthur gave it to Kay. He immediately brought the two young men back to the churchyard and had Arthur return the sword to the stone. Kay and Ector could not remove it, but the sword came out easily for Arthur.

As the young squire held it in his hands, he found his father and brother on their knees before him. Sir Ector explained that he was not his true father. The knight had not known of Arthur's royal birth—but now it was clear.

Unwilling to accept a boy as their king, many men tried pulling the sword from the stone. All failed. Time after time, Arthur pulled the

Young Arthur could do what other men could not—pull the magical sword from its stone and anvil.

sword from the stone. Still, it took many months—from Candlemas [February 2] *to Pentecost* [the seventh Sunday after Easter]—*for Arthur to finally win over the most important and powerful lords of the land.*

When at last Arthur had most of them on his side, he began to wage war against those who resisted. By force of might, he restored order to the kingdom and then made war against enemies to the north and east. Within a short time, Arthur ruled all of Scotland, Wales, and England, and peace prevailed. He built an immense castle with many towers. He called it Camelot, the grandest castle ever built. Arthur held court there and in the other great castles of his land.

Throughout Arthur's early battles, Merlin the magician was a powerful force and guide for him, helping him on many occasions.

At least once he saved Arthur from certain death. He also revealed that Arthur's end would be marked by tragedy, though Arthur did not heed or understand the warning.

The magician also helped arm King Arthur with Excalibur, the greatest sword in history. Arthur had lost his first weapon in combat and asked the magician for a new one. Merlin, mysterious as ever, brought him to the edge of a lake. While Arthur gazed out on the crystal clear water, an arm appeared with a sword in its hand. The sword disappeared, and in its place was a woman, the Lady of the Lake. When she came to him, Arthur asked if he could have the sword.

The Lady of the Lake said that the sword was hers, but she would give it to him if Arthur would give her a gift when she asked. When Arthur agreed, a boat appeared. Arthur and Merlin got in, and Arthur rowed to the arm. He took the sword, which was called Excalibur. From that day, he used it in many famous battles, slaying many foes.

The real power was not in the sword, however, but in the scabbard [sheath, or case, for a sword or dagger]. *For as Merlin told him later, "While ye have the scabbard upon you, ye shall never loste any blood, be ye ever so sorely wounded." And Arthur took his advice, keeping the scabbard as well as the sword always with him.*

It was not considered wise for a king to go out into the hostile countryside without others around to protect him. Nor was the king expected to submit himself to danger. But young Arthur's willingness to do both greatly impressed others. His fearlessness as a leader inspired his men and made them want to follow him all the more.

Knights dressed in chain mail armor (tiny metal rings linked together) prepare for battle.

—₰ SIX ₰—

THE HISTORY: CONFLICT AND VICTORY

MALORY'S FIFTEENTH-CENTURY ACCOUNT SUMMA-rized and combined much of what had been said before. Malory's beautifully written work stands as the definitive, or most important, account of Arthur's birth and reign. The wonderful legend, filled with omens and magic as well as swordplay and sin, is surely worthy of the greatest legendary king.

But if the historical Arthur lived around the year 500, his life would have been very different from the way Malory and others describe it. The magic of his birth and the swords may or may not exist in any era. But in the historical Arthur's time, there were no knights in shining armor and no tournaments.

On the other hand, there are some great similarities between legend and reality. The historic Arthur did fight many battles, which is how he gained his fame.

A closer look at the historical Arthur will help us learn more about how historians have tried to separate fact from legend. Conflict was common in fifth- and sixth-century Britain. Many small, rival kingdoms continually vied against each other. As the Roman army withdrew from Britain and the Roman system of government began to collapse, local lords and leaders became more important. Sometimes they cooperated as neighbors—trading goods, for example—but disputes arose frequently. Sometimes the rival kingdoms didn't even unite against common outside enemies.

During the fifth and sixth centuries in what later became southern England, the Britons faced several different enemies, such as the Scots and Picts (tribes or groups of families) from the north. Their most dangerous foes, however, were the Saxons. The Saxons had come to Britain many years earlier and formed an alliance with some of the local powers. In return for acting as their soldiers, local leaders gave land in southeast England to the Saxons. Disputes broke out, however, and the Britons who had been allies with the Saxons soon found themselves at war with them.

By the middle of the fifth century, the Britons had united under a king named Ambrosius and stopped the Saxon raids to the west. But the Saxons were not conquered, and they soon returned to attack.

Ongoing conflicts between Britons and Saxons are depicted in this 1850 woodcut from a medieval manuscript.

If what historians have pieced together is true, Arthur succeeded Ambrosius and commanded the British forces in battles against the Saxons. Nennius recorded those battles in the first account of Arthur, but Nennius's list is short on details. Also, the place-names Nennius used differ from modern names, which makes it impossible to be certain of the battles' locations.

Still, most historians believe that at least some of the battles Nennius describes were real and that some were Arthur's. Trying to locate them is where the detective work begins. Historians place the same battles in different sites all over England. Nearly everyone who looks at Nennius's list comes up with different ideas.

The most common interpretation has the battles extending from South Cadbury in south-central England all the way north to Scotland. Would it have been possible for Arthur to have fought over so wide an area? Historians say yes. And they have different theories to explain why and how.

They point out that the historical Arthur may have had to fight other enemies besides the Saxons. The Scots and Picts in the north and Irish tribes in the west were all enemies of the Britons. This would account for the wide-ranging list of battles.

Other scholars have skillfully used clues from archaeology and history to discover how the historical Arthur fought. Seven of the battles Nennius lists take place along rivers and two are fought on hills. It is likely that the British had horses and the Saxons did not. One historian uses this information to argue that Arthur used cavalry charges to cut off his opponents geographically. (A cavalry is an army mounted on horseback.) This might be one explanation for why Arthur's victories were overwhelming, but there is no firm proof that this was the case.

As persuasive as some of the theories seem, there is simply no hard evidence that links Arthur to any particular place, as many theorists admit. We know at least a little about one battle, however. That battle, at Badon, is the one Nennius says was Arthur's greatest victory. Historians have found it was indeed a great battle and a crushing defeat for the Saxons.

Armor and Weapons over Time

Armor is a protective covering used primarily in battle. Over the centuries, different materials, such as animal skins, bronze, and steel, were used to make armor. The design of armor changed as weapons advanced.

In prehistoric times, people used animal skins to protect themselves from clubs and axes. The Greeks and Romans wore helmets, short body armor called cuirasses, and leg armor called greaves. They also carried large shields. Greek and Roman armor was made mainly of bronze or steel to protect warriors from arrows, spears, and swords.

Animal skins

During the early Middle Ages, people used leather and chain mail—tiny rings of metal linked together—to make armor. They needed to protect themselves from arrows, swords, spears, and lances. In the later Middle Ages, when many of the legends about King Arthur were written, knights covered their bodies from head to foot.

In the 1300s, soldiers fought with crossbows, longbows, maces, and axes. Since blows from a mace or arrows shot from a crossbow could pierce or crush chain mail, armor makers, called armorers, began to use large pieces of steel to make plate armor. By the 1400s, plate armor covered the entire body—not only of the knight but also of his horse. A suit of plate armor was effective, but it was also expensive—about the price of a small farm. After armor became a safe defense, armorers began to decorate the metal for tournaments and parades. Some decoration was quite elaborate.

Bronze or steel

Chain mail

The invention of guns changed the way battles were fought and the protection that was needed. Bullet-proof armor became too heavy to wear, so soldiers ended up wearing only helmets. During the 1900s, engineers began to put armor on vehicles and ships instead of on people. By the 1960s, soldiers began wearing bullet-proof body armor that was made of strong, light, synthetic material.

In modern times, some people wear armor at their jobs. Police officers sometimes wear bulletproof vests and helmets and carry riot shields. Many athletes also wear helmets to protect their heads. Maybe you wear a helmet when you ride your bike or play a sport. Did you ever think about it as armor?

Plate armor for horse and rider

Crossbow

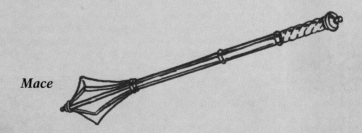

Mace

Arms and armor of a Saxon military chief

Nennius says that Arthur killed 960 men in one day at Badon. (While Nennius's words make it sound as though Arthur himself killed the men, most historians believe he means Arthur's army, not Arthur himself.) At the time, armies consisted of only one thousand to two thousand men. If the death toll is even close to correct, the battle would have been a decisive and bloody rout that should have stopped the Saxons—at least for a while.

Such a battle should have left hard evidence that historians could find in other sources, and it did. By studying the *Anglo-Saxon Chronicle*, one of the best histories of early England, historians have concluded that the Saxon raids ended for a while after the battle of Badon, which they traditionally place near the modern city of Bath, England.

We lose sight of the historical Arthur during the peaceful interlude after Badon. The scant descriptions in the *Annals* and Nennius's account provide no information about his reign or this part of his life. But it is this time that the legends celebrate. For during this peace, the legendary Arthur gathered the best knights from around the world and established the Round Table.

King Arthur's knights of the Round Table

SEVEN

THE LEGEND: QUEST FOR PERFECTION

S BOTH HISTORY AND LEGEND HAVE IT, ARTHUR was a king who proved his right to rule by battle. He fought boldly and inspired others to do so in his name. When he sought allies, he looked for those who could help him— which meant men as strong and bold as he was.

The legends tell us this led to a problem. The knights he gathered around him had strong egos to go with their strong bodies. They had killed many enemies and survived many battles, and they were used to solving disputes at the point of a sword. This method might be good during a battle, but during a time of peace, a disagreement could easily erupt into a fight between friends—especially over something as important as a knight's rank in court.

More than ego was at stake. Medieval society was structured and rigid. At the top was the king. Below the king were dukes, nobles, and knights, who together formed "the court." Far, far below them were peasants and serfs. Being close to the king brought not only prestige but also power and wealth, so rank was important.

At large feasts, the king sat in the middle of a long rectangular table, with his knights seated along the table on both sides of him.

Their places at the table were not left to chance. Usually they were determined by rank. The higher a knight was in the ranking, the closer he sat to the king.

This could lead to bloody disputes. As king, Arthur did not want his knights wasting their energy battling each other. The legends claim that Arthur established the Round Table to arrange the knights in a circle so that it would be impossible to say who was first.

In early legends, King Arthur sat apart from and above the table, since he was king and above everyone else. Later legends have Arthur sitting at the Round Table with his knights. Every chair at the Round Table was alike, and servants served every knight at exactly the same time. The knights of the Round Table represented every nationality in northwestern Europe. They were considered the best, bravest, most accomplished men.

Equality at the Round Table was the most visible sign of the code of knightly honor and behavior—called chivalry—that King Arthur and his men followed. The code of chivalry combined both military and religious ideals. A knight fought for good and against evil whenever possible. He had a deep faith in the Christian religion, showed valor in battle, and behaved honorably. The legends show that a knight never broke his promise. Courtesy to others and loyalty to one's king were also important. Every member of the Round Table upheld the code of chivalry.

Sir Kay and Sir Ector, Arthur's foster brother and foster father, were among the knights Arthur first gathered around him. Many others who helped establish his kingdom were honored with places at the Round Table. The strongest of the early knights, however, was Sir Gawain, Arthur's nephew.

Sir Gawain

Gawain's character is best portrayed in a poetic work called *Sir Gawain and the Green Knight* (author unknown), written around 1385–1390. The poem's story begins at Christmas, when a strange knight appears at King Arthur's castle in Camelot. The knight offers to let anyone cut off his head—if he is allowed a similar blow in one

This illustration of Sir Gawain appeared in the twelfth-century manuscript of Arthurian Romances *by Chrétien de Troyes.*

year's time. When none of Arthur's knights volunteers, the Green Knight mocks them. Arthur is insulted and wants to take up the challenge, but Gawain stops him. Gawain believes it is his knightly duty to face any danger for his king. Arthur tells Gawain: Hit him right, nephew, and you won't have any problem taking the return blow. Gawain delivers an enormous stroke, and the knight's head plops to the ground—where it reminds Gawain that he promised to take a similar blow. Gawain is duty bound to find the Green Knight in one year. Head under his arm, the Green Knight magically gallops away.

Although some sort of magic was at work, Gawain had given his word that he would accept the return blow, so he sets out the next year to find the knight in a green chapel in the woods. A few days before the appointed time, Gawain comes to a castle, where a lord and his wife welcome him. Gawain agrees to stay and await his appointment in the chapel, which is only a short distance away.

The lord of the castle wants to go hunting, but Gawain wants to stay behind to preserve his strength. The lord and Gawain make a deal. The lord will give him everything he catches in the woods if Gawain will give him what he gets in the castle.

Gawain agrees, thinking it's unlikely that he'll catch anything if he stays in the castle. Then he realizes the lord's wife wants to seduce him. As chivalry demands, Gawain resists her advances for three days, accepting only a chaste kiss each time. When the lord returns, Gawain dutifully gives the kisses to the lord as part of their agreement.

On his last day at the castle, the wife gives Gawain a green girdle, saying it will always keep him safe from harm. By the terms of his agreement—and the code of chivalry—Gawain should give the girdle to the lord, but knowing his head is about to be chopped off makes Gawain hesitate. He keeps the girdle, turning over only the day's kiss. He then goes to meet his fate.

The Green Knight appears in the chapel. He takes three swipes at Gawain's neck. The last is the only one to touch him, and that barely draws blood. The Green Knight reveals himself as the lord who hosted Gawain, the husband of the woman who tempted him. Sir Gawain was rewarded with his life for resisting temptation, but he was nicked in punishment for not handing over the girdle.

Gawain is ashamed of his lapse, even though he withstood the most difficult part of the test and remained chaste. The legend illustrates some of the code of chivalry. Even more important, the legend shows how difficult it can be to live up to that code.

Other knights undergo similar tests in the legends of Arthur. While they are brave and strong in battle, to be true knights of the Round

Table they must prove themselves worthy in spirit as well as in body. Arthur rewards his knights with great gifts and hosts wonderful feasts, but the true reward is simply being accepted at the Round Table.

Camelot—A Real Place?

Although Arthur and his court travel from castle to castle throughout the kingdom, his castle at Camelot remains the most majestic castle in the legends. As with the locations of the historic Arthur's battles, there have been various theories about where Camelot was located and whether it even existed.

Scholar Leslie Alcock was among those who believed it did exist. He supported a theory that Camelot was located at South Cadbury Castle in southeastern England near the River Cam. Excavations there from 1966 to 1970 showed that a fortified structure had been there during the years the historic Arthur lived. But during the digs, researchers found nothing linking the site to Arthur. His name wasn't found on any stones, for example, so the theory could not be proved.

Historians agree that the end of the fifth century and beginning of the sixth was a time of great warfare, so it is not surprising that researchers found battlements from Arthur's time. To say that they definitely belonged to Arthur would be too great a leap of logic, however. It would be like unearthing fragments from a World War I airplane in France and thinking it was flown by Baron Manfred von Richthofen, the famous Red Baron. Granted, the Red Baron flew during World War I, but without proof, such as a serial number and records showing that was his plane, we cannot conclude that the Red Baron flew that particular aircraft.

Camelot—The Ideal

In the English language, the word Camelot has come to mean an ideal place. In the 1960s, a popular musical called *Camelot* declared that life was perfect in the land of Arthur's castle. It never rained until after sundown, and life under Arthur's reign was idyllic. But the legends about Camelot and its king are much more complicated.

As the nineteenth-century poet Alfred, Lord Tennyson said in his

Guenevere and Lancelot part, as depicted in this engraving by Gustave Doré. The engraving accompanied Lord Tennyson's Idylls of the King.

Idylls of the King, "There is nothing in [Camelot] as it seems."

The legendary Camelot may be the greatest castle of all time, but even in legend it is inhabited by human beings. And no matter how hard they strive, humans are not perfect—not even Arthur. It is the legendary Arthur's flaws, along with those of his most trusted companions, that lead to his tragic end.

Excerpt from *Idylls of the King*
By Alfred, Lord Tennyson
(King Arthur addressing Guenevere)

Fear not: thou shalt be guarded till my death.
Howbeit I know, if ancient prophecies
Have err'd not, that I march to meet my doom.
Thou hast not made my life so sweet to me,
That I the King should greatly care to live;
For thou hast spoilt the purpose of my life.
Bear with me for the last time while I show,
Ev'n for thy sake, the sin which thou hast sinn'd.
For when the Roman left us, and their law
Relax'd its hold upon us, and the ways
Were fill'd with rapine, here and there a deed
Of prowess done redress'd a random wrong.
But I was first of all the Kings who drew
The knighthood-errant of this realm and all
The realms together under me, their Head,
In that fair Order of my Table Round,
A glorious company, the flower of men,
To serve as model for the mighty world,
And be the fair beginning of a time.
I made them lay their hands in mine and swear
To reverence the King, as if he were
Their conscience, and their conscience as their King,
To break the heathen and uphold the Christ,
To ride abroad redressing human wrongs,
To speak no slander, no, nor listen to it,
To honour his own word as if his God's,
To lead sweet lives in purest chastity,
To love one maiden only, cleave to her,
And worship her by years of noble deeds,
Until they won her; for indeed I knew
Of no more subtle master under heaven
Than is the maiden passion for a maid,
Not only to keep down the base in man
But teach high thought, and amiable words
And courtliness, and the desire of fame,
And love of truth, and all that makes a man.
And all this throve before I wedded thee,
Believing, 'lo mine helpmate, one to feel
My purpose and rejoicing in my joy.'

A young maiden holds the Holy Grail.

EIGHT

THE LEGEND CONTINUES:

TO SEEK THE HOLY GRAIL

T HE LEGENDS ABOUT ARTHUR MENTION MANY great battles. The legendary Arthur left England and journeyed to France, where he established his rule by fighting the local kings and then the emperor of Rome. Arthur and his knights even traveled down into Lombardy and Tuscany in northern Italy. This fantastic campaign—which could only have been accomplished in legend—finally ended in Rome. There, the pope crowned Arthur emperor.

But the true glory of the legendary Arthur and his knights came not from conquering France or even the Roman Empire, but from individual quests—adventures the knights undertook alone. There was no greater quest than the search for the Holy Grail.

The Holy Grail has come to mean the cup used by Jesus at the Last Supper, but this is not specified in the first Arthurian legends. In fact, its mystery is an important part of the stories. In the early legends, the Grail first appeared to the knights of the Round Table during a supper at Camelot that took place at Pentecost, the Christian holiday celebrating the coming of the Holy Spirit to Jesus' apostles. When all the knights were seated, thunder pealed and the earth quaked. Everyone thought Camelot itself would crumble. Then a bright beam

In legend, the Holy Grail would appear suddenly, then disappear just as quickly. This etching was created for Parsifal, *an 1882 opera by the German composer Richard Wagner. Perceval was a knight of the Round Table.*

of light entered the room, illuminating the darkness. The Holy Spirit entered each man, allowing him to see the purity of the others' souls.

And then the greatest miracle of all occurred: the Holy Grail appeared in the middle of the room, covered with a silk cloth interwoven with gold and silver. No one could see the Grail itself or who might be holding it, however. In the next instant, the Grail disappeared. In its place, the hall was filled with the favorite food and drink of each knight.

Arthur rose and gave thanks to God for the vision. Sir Gawain, though thankful, declared he could not be satisfied with the vision. He had not seen the Grail itself. As passionate as always, he swore to set out the next morning to seek it. He would not return for at least "twelve-month and a day," whatever it took to find the Grail.

Most of the other knights rose and took the same oath, and thus began the Round Table's greatest quest.

Arthur himself remained in Camelot, governing the kingdom. Though Gawain began the quest, he never succeeded in finding the Grail. The legends tell us much about the search conducted by Lancelot, the greatest knight of the Round Table, but in the end, his quest also failed.

The Greatest Knight

According to the legends, Sir Lancelot was the son of King Ban and Elayne of Benwick. He was raised by the Lady of the Lake, the same mysterious spirit who gave Arthur the sword Excalibur. In "all tournaments, jousts, and deeds of arms, for both life and death," Lancelot was the best knight of the court. Although Arthur knighted him, it was Queen Guenevere who presented him with his sword. By the rules of chivalry, Lancelot was therefore considered her knightly servant and defender. He was also a lord in his own right, with a kingdom in France.

When the quest for the Grail began, Lancelot had already defeated many knights and giants. Most of the other knights believed Lancelot would succeed in his quest, since his physical abilities were beyond everyone else's. However, there were omens from the beginning of the quest that suggested his seemingly perfect character was actually deeply flawed.

One of the omens echoes Arthur's selection as king. A sword appeared in a red marble stone magically floating in the river near Camelot. The words on the sword declared that it belonged to the best knight in the world. Arthur told Lancelot the sword must be his, but Lancelot said it was not.

Arthur urged Gawain and the others to take the weapon from the stone, but they could not. Soon a young man seeking to be made a knight appeared at court with an empty scabbard. When the knights took him to the river, he quickly drew the sword. In the tournament that followed, he beat all the knights except Lancelot and Sir Perceval, another of Arthur's favorite knights.

This illustration depicts Sir Galahad jousting during a tournament.

The young man's name was Galahad. Though Lancelot did not realize it, Galahad was his son. Lancelot had impregnated a young maiden while he had been under a magic spell, and therefore he did not know about the boy. As strong as his father, Galahad eventually proved to have the purer soul.

Body and Soul

The Grail quest belongs strictly to the legendary Arthur and his legendary court. There is no connection between the Grail and the historical Arthur. However, that does not mean that the story about the quest arose out of thin air or that it is important only as an entertaining story filled with adventure, swordplay, romance, and temptation. The story tells us a great deal about the Middle Ages and what people thought was important during that time.

Holy relics, such as the bones of or objects owned by saints, were very important during medieval times. People believed that relics had special powers that could cure disease. Possessing or even touching a relic could also help keep a person from going to hell. Since the Holy Grail was said to have held the wine at the Last Supper and was said to have been held by Jesus, Christians considered it to be among the most powerful relics.

As the legend tells us, the Grail quest is both a physical and a spiritual search, requiring both military prowess and spiritual devotion, the most important character traits of the ideal man. That was why it seemed so fitting that the ideal king should send his knights in search of the Holy Grail and why only the most perfect, sinless knight could find it. Galahad combines the qualities of strength, bravery, and piety more perfectly than anyone else. Of all the knights, he was the only one worthy enough to receive the Grail. When he did, he was taken immediately to heaven.

Why Not Lancelot?

But what of Arthur and Lancelot? Why couldn't they retrieve the Grail? We can understand Arthur not pursuing the quest, since he had a kingdom to run. After he established the Round Table, the legends tell of

Sir Lancelot is said to have been the bravest, most skillful knight of the Round Table.

him going on only one quest—and then he went in disguise. Kings were too important to ride off alone seeking adventure, which is the very nature of a quest. Besides, the stories about the legendary Arthur do not claim that he is perfect, only that he is the greatest king. He is an excellent fighter, but not the perfect knight.

Lancelot, on the other hand, had been introduced to the court as the greatest, most perfect knight of all time. His failure to retrieve the Grail, however, showed that he was flawed. According to medieval beliefs, he was guilty of a mortal sin. What was Lancelot's sin? The gravest sin imaginable—betrayal of his king, made all the worse because it was done for the highest earthly motive, love.

Queen Guenevere, King Arthur's wife, as portrayed in a painting by the nineteenth-century British artist William Morris

─── ❧ NINE ❧ ───

THE LEGEND: DISASTER

S OON AFTER ARTHUR BECAME KING, ACCORDING to the legends, a beautiful woman came to his court. The woman, Morgause, was the wife of King Lot. Lot, one of Arthur's enemies, had sent Morgause to spy on Arthur. She was also the mother of Gawain and three other boys who would grow up to become brave knights.

While under a magic spell, Arthur fell in love with Morgause, despite the fact that she was married to someone else. She stayed in Arthur's castle for only one month. When she left, she was pregnant with Arthur's son, who would be called Mordred.

Arthur did not know this at first. He also did not know that the woman was his half sister. Later, Merlin told him of this sin. At the same time, the wizard prophesied that the baby would be the destruction of the kingdom. Fearing Merlin's prophecy, Arthur banished all boys born at the time, sending them across the sea on ships. Mordred's ship wrecked, but the baby survived and was raised by foster parents. Mordred returned to the court when he was fourteen. Eventually, Arthur accepted Mordred fully, forgetting or discounting Merlin's prophecy.

In the meantime, Arthur married Guenevere. The princess was the daughter of King Lodegraunce of Camyliard and was considered to be the most beautiful woman in the world. She was slender and had fair skin and black hair. A wreath of gold leaves circled her head.

Merlin warned Arthur that the marriage would be troubled, but since the magician knew Arthur truly loved Guenevere, he didn't try to talk him out of the marriage. The ceremony was an extravagant spectacle, attended by all the great people of the day.

The "Real" Queen

Just as historians have tried to separate the historical Arthur from the legendary king, they have puzzled over his queen. While she plays a major role in the Arthurian legends, Guenevere's historic identity is even more mysterious than Arthur's.

The sixteenth-century Roman historian Boethius claimed to have seen her tomb in Scotland. If this is true, it can no longer be located. Some historians hypothesize that Guenevere was a queen in her own right before marrying Arthur and that he may have married her for political purposes. Arthur could have used the marriage to cement alliances or to obtain land, a common practice at the time.

As is the case with the historical Arthur, little remains from the time that can present irrefutable evidence about Guenevere. If the theory that she was a queen before marriage is true, however, it would explain the independence she shows in the legends. It could also explain Lancelot's devotion to her.

The Queen's Man

The legends tell us that Lancelot was Guenevere's champion. He defended her honor and completed quests in her name. Such behavior was acceptable—even admirable—according to the rules of chivalry, but it led to Arthur's downfall.

According to the legends, an enemy of Arthur's lured Queen Guenevere and Sir Kay into the woods one day and quickly overpowered and captured them. Lancelot set out to rescue them, battling not only men but enchanted lions. Along the way, he realized how great his love for Guenevere was. His love went beyond the normal bounds of chivalry or of courtly love—a pure, spiritual love.

Sir Lancelot rescues Guenevere from one of King Arthur's enemies.

When Lancelot reached the castle where Guenevere was held prisoner, he climbed the tower wall. The window to her chamber was sealed with iron bars, but he broke them. When he gained entrance to the room, Lancelot made love to Guenevere, while the injured Sir Kay slept a short distance away.

Lancelot's love was great, but he knew it was twice a sin. Guenevere was married, and they had committed adultery. Since she was married to the king, making love to her meant he had betrayed his king and committed treason. The punishment was severe—death for both of them. Guenevere would be burned alive if the truth were discovered.

This illustration (by an unnamed artist) of Sir Agravaine appeared in the fifteenth-century French manuscript Le Livre de Messire Lancelot du Lac (The Book of Sir Lancelot of the Lake) *by Gautier Moab.*

Fortunately for them, no one knew what had happened, and Lancelot vowed he would not let it happen again. He was able to resist Guenevere only by staying away from her, but eventually their love proved too strong. After the Grail quest, Lancelot found himself with the queen often. Others at court began to talk, but dared not mention their suspicions to Arthur. They feared what might happen if Arthur and his greatest knight warred against each other. The knights sensed that the kingdom and its great age of chivalry would be doomed.

The legends differ on how and why Arthur found out about the affair. According to the most popular version, Mordred was responsible. He had joined his father as a knight of the Round Table. He was jealous of Guenevere and Lancelot, however, and plotted with others to expose them.

At first Arthur refused to believe the charges. However, eventually he agreed to a suggestion made by one of the plotters, Sir Agravaine, to leave Lancelot and Guenevere alone together in the castle. When the king went out to hunt, Lancelot immediately went to see the queen in her bedchamber. "Whether they were in bed or at other kinds of pleasure," says one of the legend's authors, "I wish to make thereof no mention, for love at that time was not as love is nowadays."

Sir Mordred, Sir Agravaine, and twelve other knights gathered outside the door of the chamber, demanding that the "traitor-knight" show himself. Caught naked and expecting to die, Lancelot told Guenevere not to despair because no matter what happened, his kinsmen would not allow her to be burned. Then he went to the door. Opening and closing it quickly, he killed one of the knights and dragged him inside. He put on the dead man's armor and told those outside that if they allowed him to leave unharmed, he would submit himself to the king the next day.

Mordred and Agravaine wouldn't agree. Lancelot slew all but Mordred with single blows. Before making his escape, Lancelot urged the queen to come with him, but she refused.

Though wounded, Mordred managed to get away. He found Arthur and told him what had happened. Arthur determined that he would burn Guenevere to death, as the law demanded. Many of his knights opposed this, most especially Gawain. Few of the Round Table knights would "bear any armor to support the death of the queen." Nonetheless, Arthur planned to go through with the execution.

Lancelot, meanwhile, gathered his forces. Alerted to the queen's fate by a spy, he and his men arrived just in time to rescue her. In the tumult, Lancelot killed several good men, including Gawain's brothers. These knights had not taken up arms against Lancelot. In fact, they had tried to prevent his betrayal by Mordred and Agravaine. Their deaths were Lancelot's last break not only with Arthur but also with Gawain. Until that point, Gawain had not wanted to oppose his friend Lancelot or the queen.

Arthur set out with a huge army to besiege Lancelot's castle in France. At one point, Arthur was ready to allow Guenevere to stay with Lancelot in the hope of keeping the kingdom together, but Gawain's thirst to avenge his brothers' deaths would not allow this peace. The forces continued to fight against each other.

After many months, the pope arranged a truce. Arthur agreed to take Guenevere back and leave Lancelot alive, safe on his own land in France. Gawain had never wanted the queen harmed and supported that part of the plan. But he told Lancelot that he would see him dead.

Lancelot offered to walk from Sandwich to Carlisle, from one end of England to the other. As he walked the more than 350 miles, Lancelot promised to stop every 10 miles to found a church in memory of the slain men, but Gawain still would not make peace with him. Lancelot finally fled for his own lands in France.

Arthur and Gawain followed. The two great armies faced each other for half a year. Finally, Gawain challenged Lancelot to single combat. The fight began in the morning, when Gawain had an advantage unknown to Lancelot: a holy man had given him a gift that increased his strength every hour from nine until noon. Lancelot managed to endure the morning. When Gawain's strength began to decrease, Lancelot struck him down. Gawain's helmet rolled aside, and he waited on the ground for the death blow. Instead, Lancelot stepped back.

Gawain urged Lancelot to step forth and kill him. If Lancelot didn't do so, Gawain threatened to fight Lancelot once again. Lancelot, still as noble and chivalrous with his enemies as he had ever been, declared that he would never strike a fallen knight.

Gawain managed to recover from his wounds. As he had promised, he faced Lancelot again. They jousted with spears and finally with swords. The battle went exactly as it had the first time. Barely surviving the morning, Lancelot managed to strike Gawain's old wound in the afternoon. Again he left Gawain where he had fallen, alive but gravely hurt.

Arthur was unable to stop the fight between the two knights or the larger battle that followed. His forces couldn't break through

Lancelot's castle, and he couldn't turn the tide of the battle himself as he had in previous battles. He had lost some of his strength and ability over the years. The king by this time had become very old. Though still brave and noble, he was past his prime. The legends show that he began to react to events instead of controlling them. He was still king, but his days were numbered.

Recovering from his wounds, Gawain prepared to challenge Lancelot a third time, but he was interrupted by horrible news from Camelot. Mordred had falsely declared Arthur dead and had taken over the kingdom. Arthur and the golden age of chivalry were doomed.

At the battle of Camlann, Arthur and Mordred die.

—❧ TEN ❧—

ARTHUR:
THE HISTORIC END

T HE HISTORICAL ARTHUR AND THE LEGENDARY king intersect at the end of their reigns. There are three common reference points: the battle at Badon, Mordred, and Arthur's death. As with everything else about the historical Arthur, however, our knowledge of what really happened is hazy. Historians have had to work from faint clues and theories.

According to the *Annales Cambriae*, or the *Annals of Wales*, the historical Arthur's last battle took place at Camlann, about nineteen years after the battle at Badon. Not much else is said about the battle. It is not even clear from the *Annals* which side won or exactly where Camlann was located. No maps or signs remain from those days to show us. Nevertheless, many historians think Camlann was in southeastern England, along the natural and constructed defenses ringing the Saxon settlements.

The *Annals* declare that both Arthur and "Medraut"—whom we know as Mordred—died at the battle. They don't say whether the two men were fighting on opposite sides, and historians have debated that question.

We know that after the historical Arthur died, the British

chieftains couldn't unite to keep the Saxons permanently in check. The historian Gildas, who said he was born in the year of the battle at Badon, lamented the decline of British kings after Arthur's death. Gildas may have been correct. The Saxons eventually won all of England, though this happened long after Gildas died.

Historians have used information about the years after Arthur died to form theories about what might have happened during his life. They also have used information about common war practices during the fifth and sixth centuries. Their theories provide interesting clues about what might have happened at the end of Arthur's reign.

For example, modern historian Michael Holmes theorizes that after Badon, Arthur knew he couldn't drive the Saxons off the island, so he settled on a strategy to contain them in southeastern England. According to this theory, the historical Arthur and his allies basically conceded or gave up the area to them. This would make sense for many reasons. The Saxons had already lived there for a long time, and Arthur and the other lords might have wanted to keep them there so they could not expand their territory.

As part of the strategy, the historical Arthur would have relied on local forces to contain the Saxons. And that, Holmes and some other historians believe, could have led to his eventual downfall at Camlann.

Holmes thinks Mordred was Arthur's local ally at first, responsible for keeping the Saxons in their area. Holmes also theorizes that Mordred eventually decided to form an alliance with the Saxons instead of with Arthur. Changing alliances was common at the time, and Mordred might have seen advantages in shifting sides. When Arthur found out, he naturally would have gathered an army against Mordred to bring him back in line. The battle at Camlann was the result.

Holmes did a lot of work to arrive at this theory. He explains it in a 1996 book called *King Arthur: A Military History*. Holmes backs up his theory with arguments and evidence from other historians. He uses geography to help point out possible battle sites, and his knowledge of ancient words provides clues about Arthur's methods of fighting. Holmes uses archaeological evidence to refute other theories. He studies the *Anglo-Saxon Chronicle* to supply a framework for his theory. The *Chronicle* also helps him determine when and where battles might have taken place. His theory accounts for everything that is already known about the historical Arthur, and it accounts for some of the legendary Arthur's downfall.

All in all, the theory is a good example of how historians use legend and history to determine what might have happened in the past. Although it seems very plausible, like nearly everything else said about the historical Arthur, it remains only a theory. The facts that would prove or disprove it lie out of reach. Holmes would need an amazing archaeological discovery, such as an account written at the time or the discovery of the tombs of the soldiers killed in the battle to prove that his theory is fact.

We do know that Arthur, or someone who came to be known as Arthur, won a great battle against the Saxons at Badon. His victory kept the Saxons in check for some time, and it inspired an oral tradition celebrating Arthur's achievements. That tradition led to a great flowering of literary works establishing Arthur as a king without peer. And then, like all men, Arthur died, most likely in another great battle called Camlann.

Or did he?

Some knights of the Round Table observe Lancelot leaving Guenevere's chambers, as illustrated in French poet Chrétien de Troyes's Romance of King Arthur, *published in the twelfth century.*

——— ❧ ELEVEN ❧ ———

THE AUTHORS OF THE LEGEND

G EOFFREY OF MONMOUTH MADE ARTHUR VERY popular, and historians who first read Geoffrey used his information without question until the fifteenth century. A few historians and scholars did raise questions about the story's authenticity, but most did not conduct thorough investigations.

Meanwhile, another group of medieval writers took what Geoffrey wrote and embellished it. These are the men—and at least one woman—who rounded out the legendary Arthur. They lived in France, Germany, and England. Most of the writers made little pretense that history was more than a starting point for their stories. They were primarily interested in entertaining and educating people and exploring great ideas. They were not interested in verifying history. Writers still do this. Interweaving history with fiction is very popular with readers. Best-selling novelists such as E. L. Doctorow often choose real events as the settings for their books. For example, Doctorow based his novel *Ragtime* on events that occurred during the Roaring Twenties. Sometimes authors use real people as characters; sometimes they invent them. In their own way, modern authors are doing exactly what the medieval writers did with Arthur.

The Round Table's Inventor

Geoffrey's account, written in English in about 1135, was translated into French by 1155, a remarkably short period in those days. One of the French translators, Maistre Wace, added much description and called his work *Roman de Brut*. The name *Brut* came from Brutus, whom Geoffrey claimed was the founder of Britain.

Wace declared that King Arthur recruited the best and brightest knights of the world to be by his side. "Arthur never heard speak of a knight in praise, but he caused him to be numbered of his household," Wace wrote. Wace was the first author to write about the Round Table, explaining what Arthur did to make his knights feel equal in rank. According to Wace, the knights of the Round Table included members of every nationality in northwestern Europe. All were brave men with many accomplishments.

A Severe King

Other writers embellished Wace's work. For instance, the thirteenth-century British author known as Layamon emphasizes supernatural elements in his story. For example, when he writes about Arthur's birth, he reports that elves blessed him. In these early versions of the legend, there is no notion of chivalry. Arthur is a great warrior and king, but the justice he metes out is severe. When the Saxons break a truce, he hangs twenty-four children held hostage. This is in great contrast to the Arthur of the later stories, who would not harm a child.

Chrétien de Troyes

While Geoffrey's book was translated and enhanced, a separate group of French poets wrote about Arthur's court. Historians have connected these stories to Welsh tales, but it is difficult to sort out where the individual stories came from and to know who contributed what. A group of short poems known as the *Breton Lais* includes Arthurian tales and references to Arthur. (The term *Breton* refers to an area in northwestern France where people of British descent lived. *Lais* are poems or stories that were often composed by troubadours—lyric poet-musicians.) Among the authors of the short poems was a noble-woman known as Marie de France, who may have been connected with Henry II's court. Henry II reigned in Britain and parts of France from 1154 to 1189. He founded the Plantagenet line of British kings, which included some of England's greatest warrior-kings. They reigned during the Middle Ages.

Chrétien de Troyes wrote the most important French Arthurian works of the twelfth century. He dedicated his work to the Countess Marie, the daughter of Eleanor of Aquitaine, an important noble-woman in medieval France. Writers often thanked nobles who supported them by dedicating their works to them and their families.

Chrétien's Arthurian works include *Le Chevalier de la Charrette*, or *The Knight of the Cart; Le Chevalier au Lion*, or *The Knight with the Lion;* and *Le Conte du Graal*, or *The Grail Story*. These popular stories about knights Lancelot, Gawain, Yvain, and Perceval were written between 1170 and 1190.

Chrétien is the first writer to mention Camelot, but his contribution to the legend goes far beyond that. Chrétien's tales weave

King Henry II

different elements and themes together in a way that was new at the time. He uses the Arthurian stories to explore experiences that apply to us all, not just to powerful knights and fair damsels. One of his main themes is the power of love.

In *Le Chevalier de la Charrette*, for example, Chrétien writes about the ideal of courtly love. Great quests are undertaken in the name of courtly love. A knight might undergo many trials just to win a brief kiss on the cheek. Lancelot rescues Guenevere in Chrétien's tale, but both remain chaste. They love spiritually, not physically.

Arthur is not very important in *Le Chevalier au Lion*, a story about Yvain. The responsibilities of war and love are balanced against each other in the poem. Yvain, the hero, must atone for his sins with acts of courage and by performing great deeds. He slays a serpent and wins

An illustration in Chrétien de Troyes's manuscript shows two knights participating in a tournament in front of King Arthur, Queen Guenevere, and members of their court.

the help of a lion in his adventures. Chrétien may have been thinking of the classical Roman story of Androcles, which is about a slave
freed by a lion. He also may have gotten some of his ideas from old
Celtic legends.

Le Conte du Graal, dedicated to Marie de Champagne's cousin
Philip, Count of Flanders, was left unfinished. The story introduces
the Holy Grail and emphasizes the religious as well as the physical
demands of being a good knight. Chrétien contrasts Gawain's physical abilities with Perceval's spiritual achievements. This theme is
used frequently by later writers.

Chrétien was a great poet who mastered both style and substance.
Like other popular writers of the time, he wrote for court patrons. In
some cases, he may have chosen incidents or stories because he knew
his powerful patrons wanted to hear about them, but few other writers were able to combine different elements of the stories so skillfully. His poetry is very polished. With romance, adventure, and
pleasing morals, his stories intrigued and entertained his audiences.

More Stories

In many of the French literary works, Arthur is not characterized as
a great leader. In the thirteenth-century poem *Yder*, for example, the
king fails to give assistance to one of his vassals, which would have
been considered a grave failing. In fact, the author may have used the
story partly to insult King John, who was ruling Britain at the time
the poem was written. Still, Arthur and his knights remained popular subjects throughout France and the rest of Europe. The stories gradually moved further and further from Geoffrey's version, and they
began to involve different knights.

Lancelot is at the center of a collection of prose works called *The
Vulgate Cycle*. The tales, written in French around 1220, describe
many episodes with different themes and characters. Merlin has a
major role in the stories, as does Lancelot. These stories incorporate
Biblical traditions as well as Arthurian legends, and the search for the
Grail becomes extremely important.

In *The Vulgate Cycle*, the different knights can be interpreted as

This fourteenth-century French manuscript illustration shows Lancelot kissing Guenevere in public.

standing for symbolic virtues. In this group of stories, Arthur's death is first shown to be a tragedy, due to his own failings. These stories also introduced the Grail into the legend.

The author or authors of *The Vulgate Cycle* are unknown. Some scholars believe one author outlined the overall story, while others wrote the individual tales.

The Knights

The next great work about the legendary Arthur was *The Alliterative Morte Arthure*, which is dated between 1365 and 1400. Written in English, the poem uses alliteration to give it rhythm and richness.

Alliteration means repeating similar sounds in words. It's a little like rhyming sounds within sentences. The poem marked a new high point in the telling of the legend. Here are a few lines from the beginning of the poem, written in fourteenth-century Middle English:

> *And I sall tell [n]ow a tale [th]at trewe es and nobyll,*
> *Off the ryeall renkys of the Rownde Table,*
> *That chefe ware of cheualrye and cheftans nobyll.*

Translated into modern English, the lines mean, "I shall tell now a tale true and noble/of the real knights of the Round Table/the best of chivalry's noble chiefs."

Much of the story is still based on Geoffrey's account, but the poet (whose identity is unknown) emphasizes the exploits of Arthur's knights. In fact, sometimes Arthur is not particularly heroic, and some of his victories seem unjust. In describing the king and his court, the poet adds many details that bring the story to life, but like every writer since Geoffrey, he takes these details from his own time, the fourteenth century. Even as he looks back to Arthur's golden age, the writer describes his scenes with items from his own time period. The relationships of kings and knights, queens and ladies, the pope, wars, and arms are all more appropriate to his time than to Britain in the fifth and sixth centuries.

A Genre

By the fourteenth century, the stories of Arthur and his knights had become a genre—a category of their own. Writers wishing to tell stories about chivalry or romantic adventures would often use the knights of the Round Table. The twentieth-century novels of the *Star Trek* series are an apt, modern parallel. Often the latest books in the science-fiction series feature characters who had minor roles in earlier stories. They explore new themes and adventures to maintain audience interest, but still keep the framework set up by the original stories.

It remained for one author to sum up the legends about Arthur and his knights. Not only did he make the different tales fit together, but

Captain Kirk (right) *and Mr. Spock* (left) *starred in the original* Star Trek *series, but the stories have taken on a new life of their own. New characters carry on the* Star Trek *adventures without them. The same thing happened with King Arthur and his knights of the Round Table as Arthur stories became a genre.*

he combined their themes, too. He was a synthesizer—taking the best of everything and bringing it together in an artistic way. He would also put the focus back on King Arthur. While many of the best medieval stories about Arthur and his knights were written in French, Sir Thomas Malory, an Englishman, wove them together in his fifteenth-century book, *Le Morte Darthur*, sometimes written as *Le Morte D'Arthur*, or *The Death of Arthur*.

Excerpt from *Le Morte Darthur*
By Sir Thomas Malory

Good lord, remember ye of your night's dream, and
what the spirit of Sir Gawaine told you this night,
yet God of his great goodness hath preserved you
hitherto. Therefore, for God's sake, my lord, leave
off by this, for blessed be God ye have won the
field, for here we be three on live, and with Sir
Mordred is none on live; and if ye leave off now
this wicked day of destiny is past. Tide me death,
betide me life, saith the king, now I see him yonder
alone he shall never escape mine hands, for at a
better avail shall I never have him. God speed you
well, said Sir Bedivere. Then the king gat his spear
in both his hands, and ran toward Sir Mordred,
crying: Traitor, now is thy death day come. And
when Sir Mordred heard Sir Arthur, he ran until
him with his sword drawn in his hand. And there
King Arthur smote Sir Mordred under the shield,
with a foin of his spear, throughout the body, more
than a fathom. And when Sir Mordred felt that he
had his death wound he thrust himself with the
might that he had up to the bur of King Arthur's
spear. And right so he smote his father Arthur, with
his sword holden in both his hands, on the side of
the head, that the sword pierced the helmet and the
brain pan, and therewithal Sir Mordred fell stark
dead to the earth; and the noble Arthur fell in a
swoon to the earth, and there he swooned ofttimes.

¶There foloweth the fyrth boke of the noble and worthy prynce kyng Arthur.

¶How syr Launcelot and syr Lyonell departed fro the courte for to feke auentures / & how syr Lyonell lefte syr Launcelot flepynge & was taken. Capŧm.j.

Aone after that the noble & worthy kyng Arthur was comen fro Rome in to Englande / all the knyghtes of the rounde table reforted vnto þ kyng and made many iuftes and turneymentes / & fome there were that were good knyghtes / whiche encreafed fo in armes and worfhyp that they paffed all theyr felowes in prowelfe & noble dedes & that was well proued on many. But in efpecyall it was proued on fyr Launcelot du lake. For in all turneymentes and iuftes and dedes of armes / bothe for lyfe and deth he paffed all knyghtes & at no tyme he was neuer ouercomen but yf it were by treafon or enchauntement. Syr Launcelot encreafed fo meruayloufly in worfhyp & honour / wherfore he is the firft knyght þ the frenlfhe booke maketh mencyon of / after that kynge Arthur came from Rome / wherfore quene Gueneuer had hym in grete fauour aboue all other knyghtes / and certaynly he loued the quene agayne aboue all other ladyes and damoyfelles all the dayes of his lyfe / and for her he

i ii

A page from Sir Thomas Malory's Le Morte Darthur

TWELVE

THE LEGEND PEAKS: SIR THOMAS MALORY

N EARLY EVERYTHING ABOUT KING ARTHUR HAS been shrouded in mystery and debate, so it should come as no surprise that historians can't quite agree about who Sir Thomas Malory was. Four men have been identified as *the* Thomas Malory, though only three are in serious contention.

One was a resident of Yorkshire, England, which at that time was a county in the northern part of the country. Though a man of achievement, he is never called "Sir" in the records that remain. He was also not known to have been a prisoner. The real Malory wrote in his book that he had been a prisoner. A Malory from Papworth St. Agnes, a small village in east-central England, is often mentioned as the possible author, but he does not seem to have been a knight, as the actual Malory was.

Most authorities believe Sir Thomas Malory was a man born around Newbold Revel in Warwickshire, England, in about 1410. This Malory had been both a prisoner and a knight. He also served in France during the Hundred Years War (1337–1453). Scholars examining his book believe some of its descriptions are based on things he saw during that war. For example, Malory may have been thinking of

King Henry V

the burning of Joan of Arc at the stake as he wrote about Queen Guenevere. Also, his descriptions of Arthur, especially in the second part of the book, may have been modeled on the British king Henry V.

There is one problem, however. This Sir Thomas Malory was charged with very serious crimes, including robbery, attempted murder, and rape. Some historians find it hard to believe such a criminal could write about the perfect knight or the code of chivalry. However, other historians point out that this Malory was involved in the English civil war called the Wars of the Roses (1455–1485). They have found evidence that the crimes he was accused of may have been invented, and his only real crime may have been supporting the wrong faction in the civil war.

"The Whole Book"

Though he wrote in English, Malory used French sources for much of his work. His title for the book was *The Whole Book of King Arthur and of His Noble Knights of the Round Table*. This describes what he wrote much better than *Le Morte Darthur* does, but *Le Morte Darthur* was printed on the first copy of his book, and the name stuck. It has been used for so long that no one bothers with Malory's original title. (In keeping with the French spelling, there should have been an apostrophe between the *D* and the *a* in "Darthur," but it was not placed there in the original copy. Also, the *A* in Arthur wasn't capitalized.)

Modern prose is slightly different than Malory's fifteenth-century English. Translated into modern English, his book runs nearly seven hundred fifty pages. It brings together most of the different parts of Arthur's legend and is the version of Arthur's life most people refer to when they speak of the legendary king.

Malory was a talented author who packed his story with action and adventure. But there are other reasons *Le Morte Darthur* is considered a great work of art. In Malory's book, the king, knights, and ladies all have character flaws. Their struggles to achieve nobility and perfection add tension to the story. Malory also makes them seem more realistic by including many small details about them and their actions. Of course, the details belong to his time, not to the historic Arthur's era. Still, Malory's goal wasn't to write an accurate history. He wanted to write an inspiring legend.

Along with his writing skills, Malory had an advantage over the others who wrote about King Arthur. His handwritten manuscript found its way to William Caxton, England's first printer. In 1485, fourteen years after Malory's death, Caxton printed an edited version of the work. For the first time, hundreds and then thousands and eventually millions of people could enjoy the same story at the same time. Technology had made Arthur accessible to everyone, not just the few people lucky enough to hear a tale told at a feast or festival, or the rich man who might buy a precious handwritten copy.

Other Authors

Malory's version is regarded as a masterpiece of English literature by many critics and scholars and as an action-adventure story by those who enjoy it to this day. But other versions followed. Among the most popular was one written in the nineteenth century by English

William Caxton, the first printer in Britain, shows printed proofs to a curious audience.

poet Alfred, Lord Tennyson. It is a collection of poems called *Idylls of the King*. The poems helped inspire paintings and other versions of the legend.

Several important works of fiction on King Arthur were also written in the twentieth century. John Steinbeck, who is better known for books such as *The Grapes of Wrath* and *The Pearl*, retold Malory's story in *Acts of King Arthur and His Noble Knights*. T. H. White's *The Once and Future King*, which took twenty years to write, was a great success. His scene of Arthur pulling the sword from the stone is especially memorable.

The Mists of Avalon by Marion Zimmer Bradley takes what might be called an alternative view of both the legendary and historic Arthur. Bradley sets the story in historic Arthur's time, but tells it from the viewpoint of the court's women, especially that of Arthur's sister Morgan le Fay (or Morgaine). One of the themes of the book is the conflict between Celtic and Christian cultures. Bradley intertwines history with legend in a fresh way.

There have also been a number of plays, movies, and TV programs based on the legendary Arthur. *Camelot* is a musical (1960) and movie (1967) that loosely follows White's *The Once and Future King.* White's book was also the basis for *The Sword in the Stone,* a 1963 animated movie by Walt Disney. The movies *Excalibur* (1981) and *First Knight* (1995) both deal with the legendary King Arthur, and *Monty Python and the Holy Grail* (1975) spoofs the legend.

Meanwhile, the historical Arthur has not been forgotten. Researchers during the second half of the twentieth century did much of the work that proved Arthur really existed. One estimate in 1986 put the number of books, articles, and reviews about Arthur at 13,500, with approximately 11,000 done since 1961.

Why the Interest?

We can understand why historians and scholars are fascinated with someone considered to be the model of a perfect king. It's their job, after all, to study the past. But historians haven't been the ones who have kept the story alive. As the success of recent books and movies shows, even modern audiences want to know about Arthur—the legend even more than the real man.

Why? The story of King Arthur is an adventure story, with sword fights and wars that keep our interest and make the story exciting. The romances add spice, and the setting is exotic and far away. It seems like a time when anything can happen, especially if Merlin is walking about.

Also, the themes in the Arthurian legends are universal and timeless. One of the most important themes is the conflict between love and duty, a situation we sometimes experience in our own lives.

*Robert Goulet (left), Julie Andrews (center), and Richard
Burton (right) star in the 1960 Broadway musical* Camelot.

Another theme concerns the limitations of human beings. The knights struggle with the limits of their bodies and souls—another familiar situation for many of us. A third theme is the idea that no one is perfect. Malory combined Arthur's flaws with his greatness, demonstrating that even the perfect king is like us in many ways.

The legendary Arthur and his kingdom were undone by the king's own failings and the sin of his greatest knight. The thirst for revenge and the treachery of Arthur's own son were contributing factors, but in many ways, Arthur caused his own downfall. The end of the Round Table is Arthur's fault—a tragedy that makes us think about the nature of greatness and the nature of being human.

This illustration by Daniel Maclise appeared in an edition of Lord Tennyson's Idylls of the King. *It depicts the fatally wounded King Arthur being taken to legendary Avalon.*

—— ❧ THIRTEEN ❧ ——

A LEGENDARY END

N O ONE KNOWS WHERE THE REAL ARTHUR DIED and was buried; no monument has been found. Hundreds of years after he passed away, his body was reported to be found by monks near Glastonbury, England, but this was almost certainly a hoax. Only his name managed to survive the ruins of time, fading into the cloudy mists of human memory.

The legendary Arthur died more grandly. His remains are everywhere in literature, movies, video, and DVD. But in some ways, the descriptions of the legendary Arthur's death and the prophecy of his return echo what has happened to the historical Arthur.

The legends say that Arthur and Gawain cut short their battle with Lancelot when they heard that Mordred had betrayed Arthur. They left France and set out to win back Arthur's kingdom. They landed in the south of England, defeating Mordred's army in a great battle. But in the tumult, Sir Gawain's wounds reopened. He was found close to death. With his last ounce of strength, Gawain wrote a letter to Lancelot, reaffirming his love for his old friend and begging him to come to England and aid Arthur.

Arthur, who was greatly saddened by Gawain's death, buried him and then resumed the war against Mordred. After a frightful battle, Arthur once again emerged victorious, but the war was still not over. Arthur's conflict with Lancelot had made him many enemies in England, and Mordred was able to recruit them to his side. Nonetheless, Arthur looked forward to the next battle, believing it would be the final one. He was confident he would conquer the son who had become his mortal foe.

The night before the battle was to begin, the king had a horrible dream. He saw himself sitting on a throne in the middle of a hideous black lake, surrounded by serpents, worms, and wild beasts. He woke up just as he began to drown.

Arthur stayed awake until early dawn. Then he slept barely an instant before he had another dream. This time Sir Gawain appeared to him, as if he were alive, warning Arthur not to fight that day. Gawain told the king to delay the battle for a month, when Lancelot would return to him, and his cause would be easily won.

Arthur set out to talk with Mordred and a truce was arranged. After much discussion, they agreed that Mordred would rule Cornwall and Kent until the end of Arthur's days, when he would assume the throne of all Britain, his right as Arthur's heir.

As they arranged a meeting to sign the agreement, Arthur told his men to be careful of treachery. If they should see a flash of sword, they must attack, he told them. He did not trust Mordred to keep his word. Mordred told his men the same thing.

The meeting went smoothly, much to the leaders' surprise. Soon the two men relaxed and offered toasts of wine in celebration of the pact. As the festivities began, however, a knight was bitten by a snake and drew his sword to kill it.

The others mistook this for treachery, and the two armies descended on each other in mortal combat. Although one of his knights reminded Arthur of Gawain's prophecy, the king was overcome with anger and a desire for revenge when his men fell dead around him. Rather than retreat to safety, Arthur took a spear and ran toward Mordred. Mordred met him with a sword. Arthur's lance pierced Mordred's body. But before Mordred died, he managed to strike his father through the skull.

Some say Arthur's enemies tricked him into giving up Excalibur's healing scabbard, which would have rendered him invincible. Malory, however, doesn't mention this. He says only that Arthur was taken from the battlefield gravely wounded. Fearing he would die, Arthur gave Excalibur to his last faithful knight, Sir Bedivere, and commanded him to throw it into the lake.

Bedivere went to the lake but was tempted by the rich jewels in the sword's handle. When he returned to the king, Arthur asked if he had indeed tossed the sword into the water. Bedivere said he had.

Arthur asked Bedivere what he had seen. Nothing but waves, said Bedivere. Then you did not throw the sword, said Arthur. He commanded the knight to do so. Shamed, Bedivere returned and cast Excalibur into the water.

Sir Bedivere casts the sword Excalibur back into the lake as King Arthur commanded.

An arm caught the sword in midair, brandished it three times, then disappeared with it beneath the waves. When Bedivere reported this, Arthur had himself carried to the lake. There, a barge, surrounded by beautiful women, waited by the shore. Three queens in black garb took him aboard and slowly the barge disappeared into the growing mist, heading toward Avalon. When his wounds are healed, it is said, the legendary Arthur will return from the otherworldly island of Avalon.

But perhaps Arthur made his return long ago. For truly, he lives on in the tales told about him and the theories historians construct about his life.

The ideal of the greatest king is still as alive as it must have been during the darkest days of England. Arthur's fame has grown so great that it strides not merely over the British Isles but throughout Europe, across the ocean to America and beyond. Arthur has become a Once and Future King for all of us.

── ❧ FOURTEEN ❧ ──

BECOMING A HISTORIAN

I N A WAY, HISTORIANS ARE LIKE DETECTIVES. They learn about something that happened in the past and try to find out more about it. Who was involved? When and why did the event happen?

The past leaves many clues for good detectives. These clues may be traditions that get passed from generation to generation, folktales, works of art, archaeological objects (items that people of the past may have used in their daily lives), and books and other documents.

By doing research and studying the various clues, historians can become experts. They can frequently figure out the causes of an event, the social and cultural conditions that existed, and the political and economic events that took place. Historians can study the past to gain a better understanding about how people from other times thought and acted, but they can also learn from past thoughts and events and use them as a guide for making decisions. Sometimes historians disagree with each other even after doing similar research.

How does a beginning historian get started? Start with what other historians have written. Go to the library and ask the reference librarian to help you find bibliographical information. A bibliography is a written record of books, manuscripts, and articles used in creating a particular work. It tells people what sources an author used when he or she was doing research. The bibliography in this book would be a good place to start if you want to learn more about the life and times of King Arthur.

SELECTED BIBLIOGRAPHY

Alcock, Leslie. *Was This Camelot?* London: Thames and Hudson, 1972.

Ashe, Geoffrey. *The Discovery of King Arthur.* New York: Doubleday, 1985.

Barber, Richard. *King Arthur: Hero and Legend.* New York: St. Martin's Press, 1986.

Bradley, Marion Zimmer. *The Mists of Avalon.* New York: Ballantine Books, 1984.

Foss, Michael. *The World of Camelot: King Arthur and the Knights of the Round Table.* New York: Sterling Publishing Co., 1995.

Geoffrey of Monmouth. *The History of the Kings of Britain.* Translated by Sebastian Evans and revised by Charles W. Dunn. New York: E. P. Dutton & Co., 1958.

Goodrich, Norma Lorre. *Guinevere.* New York: HarperCollins, 1991.

Goodrich, Norma Lorre. *King Arthur.* New York: Franklin Watts, 1986.

Hodges, Margaret. *Knight Prisoner.* New York: Farrar, Straus and Giroux, 1976.

Holmes, Michael. *King Arthur: A Military History.* New York: Barnes & Noble Books, 1996.

Hunter Blair, Peter. *Roman Britain and Early England.* New York: W. W. Norton & Company, 1963.

Lacy, Norris J., ed. *The Arthurian Encyclopedia.* New York: Garland Publishing, Inc., 1986.

Malory, Sir Thomas. *Le Morte Darthur.* Edited by R. M. Lumiansky. New York: Macmillan Publishing Company, 1982.

____. *Le Morte Darthur*, Vol. 2, *Romance.* Edited by Ernest Rhys. London: J. M. Dent & Sons, Ltd., 1906.

Matthew, Donald. *Atlas of Medieval Europe.* New York: Facts on File Publications, 1983.

Matthews, John, ed. *An Arthurian Reader.* London: Aquarian Press, 1988.

Roberston, D. W., Jr. *A Preface to Chaucer.* Princeton, NJ: Princeton University Press, 1962.

Steinbeck, John. *Acts of King Arthur and His Noble Knights.* New York: Farrar, Straus and Giroux, 1993.

Tennyson, Alfred. "Idylls of the King." In *Complete Poetical Works.* Boston: Houghton Mifflin, 1963.

White, Richard, ed. *King Arthur in Legend and History.* New York: Routledge, 1998.

White, T. H. *The Once and Future King.* New York: Putnam, 1996.

★ ★ ★

Website:

The Camelot Project at the University of Rochester, New York. September 7, 2000. <http://www.ub.rug.nl/camelot> (December 31, 1998). This site contains numerous texts related to Arthur, including translations of Geoffrey of Monmouth and summaries of some of the basic characters. It also includes an excellent bibliography.

SOURCES

9   The description of the historical Arthur is drawn primarily from Michael Holmes, *King Arthur: A Military History* (New York: Barnes & Noble Books, 1996), 106–132.

9   The historic background is drawn primarily from Peter Hunter Blair, *Roman Britain and Early England* (New York: W. W. Norton and Company, 1963), 149–167.

9   Holmes, 113.

10   Ibid., Leather armor.

11   Nennius, "Historia Britonum" (History of the Britons), translated and excerpted in Richard White, *King Arthur in Legend and History* (New York: Routledge, 1998), 4–5.

11   Holmes, 112.

14   Norris J. Lacy, ed., *The Arthurian Encyclopedia* (New York: Garland Publishing, Inc., 1986), 494.

19   Lacy, 479–494.

20   Richard White, 4–5.

20   Richard Barber, *King Arthur: Hero and Legend*

(New York: St. Martin's Press, 1986), 4.

20 Nennius, in Richard White, 4–6.

20 Barber, 6.

21 Ibid.

22 See the date published in *The Annals of Wales,* in Richard White, 6. Among others, Michael Holmes prefers an earlier date at the end of the fifth century (Holmes, 90–91).

22 Richard White, x.

22 Ibid., 7.

22 Holmes, 1.

25 Barber, 8, 1–16.

27 Ibid., 28–30.

28 *Webster's New Biographical Dictionary* (Springfield, MA: Merriam-Webster, Inc., 1988), 393.

28 Lacy, 209.

29 Barber, 25.

29 Richard White, 25.

29 Barber, 37.

29 Geoffrey of Monmouth, *The History of the Kings of Britain,* translated by Sebastian Evans, revised by Charles Dunn (New York: E. P. Dutton & Co., 1958), 170–236.

30 Ibid., 234–236.

33 The account of Arthur's beginnings are drawn from Sir Thomas Malory (R. M. Lumiansky, ed.), *Le Morte Darthur* (New York: Macmillan Publishing Company, 1982), 3–97.

34 Ibid., 5, 8.

37 Ibid., 37.

40 Hunter Blair, 149–167.

40 Gildas, *The Ruin of Britain,* in Richard White, 90.

41 Holmes, 109.

41 Ibid., 112–116, 132, 1–2.

41 Nennius, in Richard White, 5.

45 Holmes, 92.

48 Richard White, 45.

48 *The Concise Columbia Encyclopedia* (New York: Avon, 1983), 167.

48 Richard White, 438.

48 "Sir Gawain and the Green Knight," in *The Oxford Anthology of English Literature,* Vol. I (New York: Oxford University Press, 1973), 284–348.

51 Leslie Alcock, *Was This Camelot?* (London: Thames and Hudson, 1972).

52 Alfred Lord Tennyson, *Idylls of the King* (New York: Thomas Y. Crowell

and Company, 1885).

53 Ibid.

55 Malory, 119–137, 131, 38, 528-532.

56 Ibid., 528.

57 Ibid., 81, 141.

57 Richard White, 274.

57 Malory, 521–575.

63 Ibid., 28–38, 63

64 Norma Lorre Goodrich *Guinevere* (New York: HarperCollins, 1991), 23.

64 Malory, 63.

64 Goodrich, 9, 19–44.

66 Malory, 627–729.

67 Ibid., 696, 697, 704.

68 Ibid., 711, 720.

68 From Malory, 726–727.

71 *Annales Cambriae,* in Richard White, 6.

72 Gildas, in Richard White, 6.

72 *See* Holmes.

72 Ibid., 149–151.

73 Ibid., 148.

75 Barber, 27, 37.

76 Ibid., 38–39.

76 White, 45.

76 Robert Wace, "Brut," excerpted and translated in Richard White, 46.

76 Barber, 41–54, 55–56.

79 Ibid., 62.

79 Richard White, 162.

79 Ibid., 241, 271.

80 Barber, 74–75, 73.

81 Richard White, 96–97.

81 Barber, 43–45.

82 Sir Thomas Malory, *Le Morte Darthur,* Vol. 2, *Romance,* edited by Ernest Rhys (London: J. M. Dent & Sons, Ltd., 1906).

85 The discussion of Malory's identity is based on Barber, *King Arthur: Hero and Legend,* 114–116.

85 Barber, 114.

86 Margaret Hodges, *Knight Prisoner* (New York: Farrar, Straus and Giroux, 1976), 104–123.

86 Barber, 115, 117.

87 For example, see Malory, *Le Morte Darthur.*

87 *Webster's New Biographical Dictionary,* 185.

87 Hodges, ix.

88 Barber, 194.

89 Marion Zimmer Bradley, *The Mists of Avalon* (New York: Ballantine Books, 1984). See page 317.

89 Barber, 199.

93 Arthur's end is summarized from Malory, *Le Morte Darthur,* 730–741.

INDEX

ABOUT THE AUTHOR

Besides a biography about Joan of Arc, Jeremy Roberts's recent nonfiction books include works on skydiving and rock climbing. He's written several installments in the Eerie, Indiana series and quite a few horror tales. His adult books include a historical trilogy and techno-thrillers. He lives with his wife and son in a haunted farmhouse in upstate New York.

Illustration Acknowledgments: © The Art Archive, pp. 2–3; © The Granger Collection, New York, pp. 8, 16, 49, 86; © Minneapolis Public Library and Information Center, p. 10; © Charles Walker Collection/Stock Montage, Inc., p. 12; the map on page 15 is by Tim Seeley; © Hulton Getty/Liaison Agency, Inc., p. 18; © Stock Montage, Inc., pp. 21, 32, 58, 88, 95; © North Wind Picture Archives, pp. 24, 38, 40, 44, 56, 77, 84; © Mary Evans Picture Library, pp. 26, 35, 52, 60, 92; © Michael Nicholson/CORBIS, p. 28; © British Tourist Authority, p. 30; © Bettmann/CORBIS, p. 46; © Tate Gallery/The Art Archive, p. 62; © Mary Evans Picture Library/Edwin Wallace, p. 36, 65; © AKG Photo London, p. 66; © Mary Evans Picture Library/Arthur Rackham Collection, p. 54, 70; © Gianni Dagli Orti/CORBIS, pp. 74, 78; © Bibliothèque Nationale Paris/The Art Archive, p. 80; © Photofest, pp. 82, 90.

Front cover: © Richard T. Nowitz/CORBIS.
Back cover: © Ted Spiegel/CORBIS.